AF333532

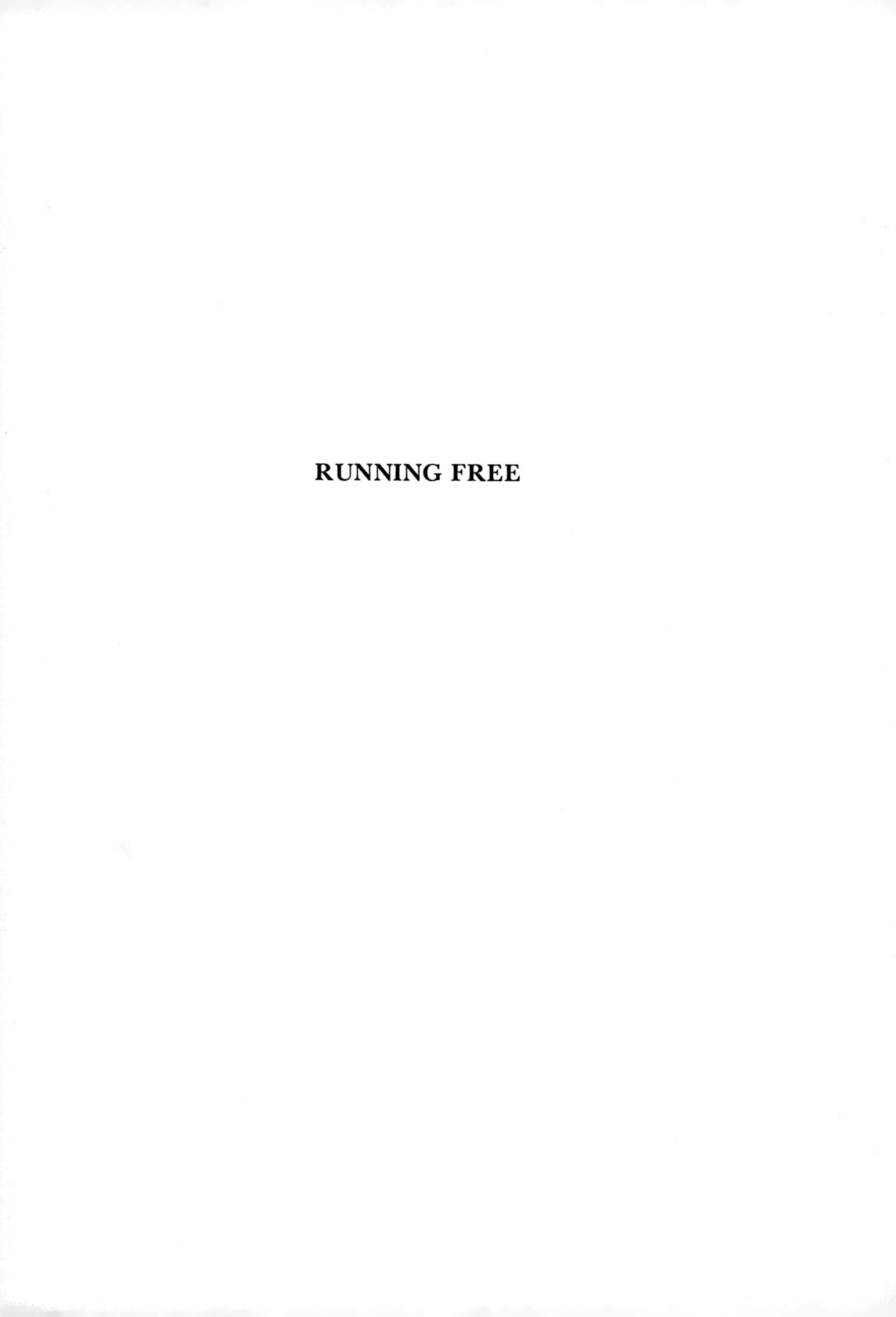

RUNNING FREE

Library of Congress Catalog Card Number 75-22930

ISBN 0-8233-0229-6

Printed in the United States of America

MARGARET GUENTERT

Running Free

THE GOLDEN QUILL PRESS
Publishers
Francestown   New Hampshire

To Cac and Ruth

ACKNOWLEDGMENTS

Grateful acknowledgment is made to the following in which some of the poems included in this book were first published: *The Archer, Poetry of Our Time, Orphic Lute,* and *The Lark and the Sky.*

My appreciation to Mary Ellen Moore for typing the *Running Free* manuscript and to Sara Alley, Jeanne Dille, and Eileen Parris for proofreading it.

CONTENTS

RUNNING FREE

A PIECE OF PAPER

A piece of paper, blank, damp,
Sticks to my jacket pocket.
I tucked it there this morning,
Hoping to record an idea while I sailed.
Pockets like sequestered rooms
Grow cluttered and musty.
They are storage places for the unnecessary
When the sun shines and the wind beckons.

There were ideas, ideas worth recording.
The sea reminded me
That power can be gentle,
That elemental stings nourish fortitude,
That gulls transcend motors and sails.
The shore harbored Irish moss and sea lavender.
Kelp pulled at the rudder:
The bold can overshadow the delicate, but not
    destroy it.

The paper lies in a heap with the kleenex and
    the matches.
The ideas live.
In March when the paper is ash and the jacket
    is stored,
I will recall the wind.

CLOUD SHIPS

Cloud ships weigh anchor at sunset,
Their masts paralleled to heaven.
A gray veil shades the sun's descent,
Scatters golden light.
Motley spinnakers harness spilling rays.
Pink sails pull the wind to earth.
The ship glides through the fathomless sky
Into the mist, night.

REFLECTION

Years ago I clipped a photograph
Of moonlight on a cold, dark bay.
Was it accident or blind-sight
That I chose a picture I'd see one day?

In August when summer grew to its end,
I walked by the shore one night.
I saw the moon, a craft alone,
Hovering. I remembered the light.

What camera had captured the tone,
The scope of the sea and the sky?
What f/stop could control the time,
What lens absorb the diminished rays
Rising on waves, falling in bends?
What truth snaps the moment of my delight?

SUNSET

The sand slapped my face,
Forbade me to stroll in leisure,
Showed me I walked alien ground and
Had to defend myself before the monarch
   wind.
I squinted and stumbled on,
Determined to watch the sunset
By the sea.
The water lapped near my feet
As if to warn a stranger of his foe.
The wind rose to the hills.
I viewed the purple west
For an instant — well worth the war
With the wind.

DESIGNS

A force beyond the earth controls the tides
Invisibly. The stress maintains the flow:
The undulating current always rides
Between contending orbs of potent glow.
Alone I climb the rocks; I watch the sea,
The sky that holds the movement I define.
Alone I wonder at the mystery,
Concern of modern science, ancient rhyme.
A force beyond my ken invades my heart
To turn my thoughts from universal laws
To driftwood, gulls, and tidepools, nature's art.
Within these bounds I wonder still the cause
For motion and the reason of design
In air, in sky, in water, and in time.

LITTLE DOUBTS

Little doubts
Gather
Like storm clouds.
Thunder echoes through the land.
Torrential fear dashes faith,
Exposes weak roots,
Erodes the will,
Levels men and the nation to the
  dusty plain.

THE PRIVILEGE

The land is no longer ours
Nor was it ever.
Once we thought toil
And love were the bases for a claim.
We have returned to find
The sun casting a dim light
From the western sky.
Dry, brown leaves cover the fertile ground.
The claim is memory.
It knows no season.
It alone can prevail
Over the privileges of time.

OUR FIRE

You blew and from seemingly dead ashes
Came a strand of smoke.
I ran to fetch fuel from our full woodpile.

We watched the blue flame battle the orange one.
It was an endless war, but it was not our war.
And it was a better show than the usual late movie.
The air was fresher too: salt savor and pine, not
    stale smoke.

Here no wall enclosed our dreams:
They were free to explore the dark air,
To come and go at will,
Protected from half-hour chimes, city nightmares,
    and backyard fences.

We settled against a tree stump.
I saw the frost glitter on the grass
Near our fire in the cove.
There was a chill that night.
At home we would have added a blanket,
Though by our fire we knew a stronger warmth.

NORTHERN LIGHTS

The phantom dancer in the sky
Wears silver shoes, a silver gown.
In August she will never die,
Rising, fading among the clouds,
Caring not that the moon is down.
Her raiments change without reason.
She comes suddenly into view
In pale green on the horizon,
In pink leaping to the zenith,
Bowing to the west in bright blue.
An encore she begins.
She moves through shadows in the north,
Fading, rising, fading again.

INVERNESS REVISITED

The night has no sound.
Crickets cry.
Trains wail and intimidate
The nostrils of the crowds they pass.
Tunnels amplify the monotonous trails of steel.
A breeze wrestles the rust on the fencepost,
Blows away the harshness of day,
Relieving the eyes, allowing the skin to breathe.
When darkness falls, spirits live.
They survive on the primal diet, fear.
I reach out. I see outlines of matter.
I remain confused in the night which has no sound.

FIREFLIES

Down dark paths
Ideas flit like fireflies
Casting a fanciful glow.

QUANTITY "X"

X equals the unknown.
X is chi.
X equals a crossroad.
What leads to *X*?
Question: When did *X* come to be?
XXX — a child writes under his autograph.
Time, language, direction —
X means nothing;
X means everything.

POLYPHEMUS

From out his cave
He comes to rave,
Teratoid thunder loose on the track.

A hollow wail
From the rigid trail
Warns that he moves without sight.

In station dim
I wait for him
To rip through the fearsome black.

Straight and sure
With tedious roar,
Polyphemus streaks through the night.

LEECH

A leech can heal:
Praise leeches,
Blood-belly full,
Wallowing in weak flesh,
Limply resisting detachment.
Who can tell when the parasite's poisoned will
Permeates the calculations of learned men?

Pull, pull the soft treachery:
Too much letting will kill.

THE MISTAKE

We laugh at the mistakes —
    Bent fenders,
    Weeds in the garden,
    Soggy apple pie.

We laugh at the
    Children playing,
    Words spoken and unspoken,
    Fear of lightning when the storm has
        passed by.

We laugh at
    Baffled men,
    Broken promises,
    Unplanted seed.

We laugh
    In the light when the kite will not fly,
    But in the night
    I cry.

LOLLIPOPS

Lollipops were special once,
And my swing, newly exciting everyday.
The grass was cool and soft that June day
And balloons floated half way to the sun.
A fuzzy, blue rabbit wrinkled his nose
    when we were alone:
What friends we were!

My swing broke during a September storm.
It is December. I have a shriveled
Balloon in my pocket. The
Blue rabbit is
Dirty and no longer wrinkles
His nose, not
Even when we
Are alone.
But lollipops were special
Once.

BUILDING BLOCKS

A boy would fashion his perfect world in blocks.
Piece by piece with symmetry it grows
(The foundation alone consuming an hour's effort).
Time out for lunch —
The swish of a collie's tail —

There'll be more days,
More blocks,
More tails.

GODS' EYES

Poetry and friendship are names I have learned.
Puzzles and crafts are time-passers I know.
Eyes measure love in earth-bound cases.
Eyes measure love.

Friends share language,
Share puzzles and crafts.
Eyes measure love in time-bound places.
Eyes measure love.

Weave language. Weave friendship.
Weave gods' eyes by the skein.
Eyes measure love in human faces.
Eyes measure love.

WORLDS

Arthur Clarke knows worlds
That may not be,
Worlds that the informed can imagine
In 1973.

George Orwell knew a world
That may be,
A world that the informed will abhor
In 1984.

Hamlet knew worlds
That last forever,
Worlds that are and will be
In men's hearts.

I know worlds
Neither great nor real,
Worlds of color and of sound.
I know them.

Imagination works
In time far and near.
Men die and others mark it
With an indelible tear.

CIVILIZE

Lesotho, civilize Lesotho.
Destroy savagery with sanitation and the
    Word.

Travelers will tour
Red, mud huts one day
As they tour grass huts
And tepees now.
They will stay at the Maseru Hilton
In air-conditioned rooms
When primitive tribes are won,
When advances come
To the backward, happy land.

THE PATIENT MEN

A forest surrounds them.
They are brave men
To have carved a niche in civilization,
A sequestered Eden in the wilderness.
Inside the fence they wait,
Pacing and pacing, day after day.
It is a hopeful existence.

The parcel will come someday
(They have been patient for years).
Inside will be magnificent peace,
Sequel to Pandora's treasure.

THE PARADE

Rain, mud, snow, sun
Pass,
Come

Days, weeks, months, years,
Pulse beats,
Tears

Parade of people —
Smiles,
Frowns,
Hope,
Let down.

One —
Just one —
Brings meaning.

IN TIME

The plane nears Hilo.
The big island emerges
From the sea.
One gets the color
Of Hawaii, a view
That the sun enhances
In its retreat to be
On time in Japan.

LOVE

Love grates painfully
Like a grain of sand
Within the heart.
There grows no pearl,
But, in defense, sometimes a poem.

POETRY LIVES

Poetry lives on the second floor
Of a fishing shack by the river.
A man casts bait before dawn.
He waits.
Some days he gets only a nibble.
Some days he sleeps on the shore.
Sometimes the weather beats his dream.
Once in a while he lands
Food for Solomon and Shakespeare.
After dark the fragrance of the fry
Drifts in the wind.
Poetry lives on the second floor.

SMALL FINGERS

Small fingers pull at the wheat.
Grains tumble across a tiny hand
Onto the ground.
A tern, soaring,
Reaps the wonder in the young eyes,
Gray as the lake of ten-thousand autumns.
Threats of October frost bring harvest
Of the wheat, the tern, the child.
A warm wind sows new seeds in another spring.

NOVEMBER

Something in your eyes —
Historic,
    Profound,
        Eternal —
Hinted at it:
Ships leaving the harbor,
    Hope for the home port,
        Destruction at sea;
Gulls circling at dawn,
    At sunset,
        Forever in the mind;
A child awed by a butterfly,
    Youth,
        Fulfillment;
Spring soil after the rain,
    Wheat,
        Harvest;
The pied hills of October,
    A recession of color,
        Rich November.

WITHIN

Within the icy stream I see
Reflections of the sky.
In sunset's rays a hundred thoughts
Of springtime ripple by.
The cold March water animates
A memory of the sea,
Of other days, of magic waves
That chill less bitterly.
Yet here I wander in the mist,
Dead reeds my company
In prayer to the listless wind —
Awaken harmony.
Approaching clouds gather in
The faded yellow light
To save the rays in caverns dim
Despite ensuing night.

SIGNS

The signs point the way:
"Slow,"
"Speed Kills" — the body or the mind?
"Stop" — live?
"Yield" — to what?
"Go" — where?
"Caution" — of course, always caution!
"Exit" — we must sometime.

A MOMENT

I think I saw his image
Reflected on the wet pavement.
Perhaps I heard him.

I felt a moment of summer sun.
Then all was dark and silent again.

NO WORDS

No words,
No important words;
Feelings,
Transcending the silence in a drifting canoe,
Spotlighted by the moon.

PRELUDES

Odysseus sails for home, trials won,
To faithful Penelope, to his son.
In a ten-year test of his strength and wits,
He beat Poseidon with indirect hits.

When Chaucer's Pardoner and Wife of Bath
Exchange hypocrisies, the world can laugh:
When pilgrims spin their tales to pass the time,
One hears across the years the human rhyme.

Prelude of solemn bass and violin,
Bach's mood, "O man bewail thy grievous sin."
"Come my joy" permeates the passion some speak —
Ethereal, the strings and chorus meek.

Swells break in surf, varied in shape and sound.
Ideas break in languages profound.

THE NEW YEAR

In 1949 I watched the ball drop above Times Square.
A half century ended;
A half century began.
The crowd cheered the fading despair of recorded time,
The hope of unknown history.
I cheered the occasion: I was nine.

Twenty three years later (the ball has marked the time)
With Milton's doubt and faith,
I remember Times Square.

Other symbols have marked endings and beginnings.
The eves and dawns pass
Quietly when I am alone in celebration.
I cheer the occasions
When despair ends, when hope begins,
When I am again a child of nine.

SPRING SEED

A spring seed carried by wind and water,
Only the firm ground,
Chilled from the winter ordeal
Could hold me.

Its grasp was terrifying;
It gave an edgy security to my naiveté;
I knew its depth and power so I stayed
To fulfill my destiny.

I grew strong; I looked steady:
My roots had penetrated rich soil.
I could look to the earth only occasionally
(Pride demanded aloofness of me)
Though in silence we both knew the relationship.

LAHAINA

No brown leaves clutter the streets of Lahaina;
No snow falls there.
The whaling village rests in the September sun
Waiting for the season,
Waiting for the whales to come.

Palms dance in the wind in Lahaina.
One Banyan tree shades
The square from the tropic sun.
Above the town, West Maui Mountain
Lives in ever-present rain.

The land and the people grow together,
Except when the missionaries
Criticize the weather,
The waiting for the season,
The waiting for the whales to come.

STRANGERS

They were twenty.
One day the wrinkles began.
What does that man
   By the window
      Think about
         As he
            Dozes
               In the afternoon?
What does he know
That years of hope and pain will teach me?
What dreams droop
   In the head of the thin lady
      Who paces all day?
Are they
My dreams
   With sixty years added?
The old ones smile,
Strangers
Who know but cannot tell.

TOMATO PATCH

The ground thawed.
It welcomed the feet it had regarded
As intruders in the snow.
Dull greens brightened,
First along the fence,
Later in the whole yard.
The old tomato patch stood
As a graveyard of paupers' crosses,
Rough, gray stakes, some upright, others bent,
Some with dead vines clinging,
Others bare,
All at odds with the green world;
They would remain that way,
A monument to the death of one who cared,
A scar recalling the full cycle.

THE BRIDGE

I stand near the bridge to a new land
On the spot where I came to understand
Why men fail, yet live, and why they smile.
The spot, which I cleared of trees, became
My refuge from imagined pain,
A whey-faced witch, and other unknown demons;
My habitat for mind-born pleasures
Emerging from a cavern of treasures
Stored to nourish an independent soul;
My hearth where one kindled in me
The courage to build and to be.

One day I left that part of the wood
To search for other sites where I could
Gaze beyond the trees and the well-known stream.
I saw the cities; I saw the seas.
In books I read the mysteries
Of space, of time, of human spirit.
I understood as little then as now.
I loved the song of wind in bough,
Of wave on rock, of bird at dawn.
I loved the song of man, the melody
Of courage to build and to be.

I stand near the bridge to a new land
Feet unsteady on banks of sand.
I must leave the familiar wood again
To travel to an unknown shore.
Will I find in its shelter the core:
The wind, the wave, the bird, the melody?

AFTERWARD

Pine scented embers glow in the grate.
Who laid the fire?
Who struck the match?

I remember blowing the spark
Until I was dizzy.
The flame finally rose
To mock cold feet,
To hypnotize the guests,
To nip the chill of August.

Melted ice,
Ashes,
Uncertainty
Live in the dark room.

THE BRANCH

Broken, yet it clings to its sustenance.
Life begins to flow, and even a multitude
    of alienation cannot destroy
    one thread of association.
Look, a bud testifies to the power of will
To live.

ROADS

I have traveled enough roads
Marked "dead end" to know there is nothing
    there.
When I read the sign,
I continue on my "no outlet" way
To an abandoned promise,
Beaten by the rain,
Forgotten in thruway traffic,
Open to me.
I have traveled marked roads,
And I will again.
Hope shines through dust.
I move along, and must,
Whatever roads I find.

PROBLEMATIC

The new man Adam finds his city fair,
Civilized-safe from old temptation's snare.
What demon serpent from his rustic lair
Would venture down a modern thoroughfare?
The new man Adam asks his questions now:
Why my son Cain? He could not help the row?
Such injustice the law should not allow.
Well, I object and Eve objects, but how
Can we convince some judge who wasn't even
    there.

SEAS

Ernest Hemingway sailed the sea.
He imagined Ernest Hemingway sailing the sea.
Eighty-four days without a catch,
A cruise to lands little known,
He sailed in search of home.

Joseph Conrad sailed the sea.
He imagined the universal soul
Adrift in the world,
Primal causes in British domain;
Conrad wrote of Eden and Cain.

Herman Melville sailed the sea.
He imagined a personal dilemma
("Let Ahab beware of Ahab") and certainty
    ("Call me Ishmael").
He knew the sea.
"And I only am escaped alone to tell thee."

SUMMER STORM

From ebbing mist evolves the golden sea,
Created by the spotlight of the dawn;
It shines to tempt the workman's weary mind —
In warning clouds too soon is grandeur gone.

Gray mercenaries march across the sky;
They cast a gloom amidst the lustrous waves.
With stealthy, steady sweeps, they snatch the gold.
Loud thunder sounds the booming victory praise.

The wind commands the stratagem of storm,
Spectacular in power, wide in scope.
Dramatic battles rage above, below
As clashing clouds and waves both act in hope.

Now nature aptly executes her schemes:
Gray shadows steal the gold of ocean dreams.

RAINBOWS

A rainbow follows summer storms
That sun intrudes upon. After
The thunder dies, Apollo warms
The earth with rays, celestial laughter.

Reapers' hopes live in the land,
Nourished by change of season,
Harvested by toil, and planned
For the support of faith and reason.

Some castles lie along the shore
Where tides tear at dreams
Conceived in concrete cities,
Constructed in sand with driftwood beams.

Whatever seems gentle, whatever raw,
In Nature's congress order writes the law.

CASTLES

The children of the world build castles in the sand.
Each morning the sun rises on ruin:
The waves smash the moat, the tower.
The tide steals a young dream.
The children of the world begin again
On a new day with new warmth and new plans:
This castle will surpass the one
They fashioned yesterday.
The sailor knows the cruelty of the sea,
The skill he needs to venture on the main.
He works to win a battle with the waves.
Storm and wind bend his hope in lashing rain.
The sailor stays alert astride the beam.
Children of the world continue the dream.

TIDEPOOLS

Waves lash the island, shape her as they will.
Tides flood stately rocks, smooth the sharp corners,
Leave the deep's dead refugees in the spill.
Limpets and algae remain as mourners
Along the shore. Tidepools, earth's little seas,
Collect pieces from the ocean's fury.
They hold in miniature colonies
Life in pause from its natural hurry.
Retreating from an ordinary day,
I watch the waves, the diminutive sea —
The living, the dead, the colors, the grey —
Listen in leisure to sad harmony.
In the mist of time in pauses I find
Endless tidepools of the shore, of the mind.

WINDWARD

A ship drifts out; no billows fill her sail.
Harbor mist, at odds with the sunrise glow,
Shrouds her glory in white-light, dim and pale.
Lapping water comforts the idle prow,
Gently asserts the strength of the sea,
Iridescent with hope, gray with despair,
Tempting with fathomless mystery,
Profound in furtive stillness, new dawn's air.
There is a plan: a helmsman gives command
To lift the sail windward beyond the bay.
What new adventure lies within the main?
The sun will rise; the mist will burn away
Above the rolling sea that touches land,
Batters and lifts the ship, the hope, the day.

CIVILIZATION

As wars blaze and men lie,
Civilization seems a scab on a seething sore
That some god poked in Nature
With his fertile sword eons ago when man began.

Ugly thing, a scab, but lucky —
Dike-strength against a natural excess
That would flow and flow and still be excess.

Does the wound heal?
Will the patient die?
Will some Harvey explain the process?

With the need of a boy, skinned-kneed,
The wounded looks at his sore,
Gains comfort from its cover,
(Possible through the efforts of Eli Whitney, *et. al.*).

Where is that fertile sword?
Where is that god
Who fails to deliver his punch line?

FORECAST

The simplicity of the electric age
Eludes the simplicity of the past.
Mozart's music, Rousseau's rebellion,
Shakespeare's heroes, Thoreau's principles
May fade.
Plato's cave will remain;
A plug can be installed
To warm the inhabitants
Should the sun fail.
Electricity simplifies, negates
Confrontation. Old tyranny yields
To new tyranny.
The soul grows closer to the body
(Perhaps there is a soul).
A voice without the aid of a plug
Cries.
I listen;
The message impels me;
The medium commands my heart.
How simple.
One sound reaches through time.
How simple.
Cloudy skies, ten percent chance of snow.

IN THE HOUSE

Here we are, dog,
You and I in the empty house
Wringing silence from the drapes,
Watching for a breeze in the painted meadow,
Searching for a magazine, for warm milk,
For an ash tray, for a footstool, for a bone,
For something.
The memories are in the attic
In flaking cartons and splintery boxes,
All ordered for eternity.
And the meaning must be beyond that cold, outside
    wall.

CLUTTER

An unanswered letter on a box of paper,
Seven bills (unpaid),
A nailfile,
A dry pen,
A book I "must" read,
Notes of events, appointments, and encouragement,
An ink-stained report,
A dictionary: "Will-o-the-wisp" follows "willing."
There was a poem, my poem —
It must be here —
A cluttered desk, a cluttered life,
And all I want is at the bottom of the pile.

INVISIBLE FORCES

There was a void where invisible forces died.
The tarnish on unused armor
Turned to rust in a dark cavern.
The pain of unopened wounds
Burned in my back, my head.
The tears for a loss that would not be
Dried on a scorched plain.
You came.
I knew we'd bend the shield
When we joined the fight,
But the mask would glisten in the sun.
Gashes would open and be healed.
Tears would fall in the night
On a pillow where your head had been.

CAPTIVE OF THE NIGHT

I watched in silence.
All that remained of the summer
Glistered in the moonlight,
Captive of the night, in the waves.
When the sun rose in June,
I tried to imagine the days ahead.
But who can? Who can?
They passed as each morning passes,
As a lifetime passes.
Evening came.
What distant terror dances
In the moonlight on a dark bay?

RUNNING FREE

The sun flashes against the mast,
Blinds me until waves sway the prow.
Spray showers the cockpit. Holding line fast,
I tug at joy, all the wind will allow.
A gull calls his claim for a fish;
He swoops for the catch along port.
The seals rest on their island in the mist
Watching what passes like jurors in court.
Beyond the island lie three miles of sea,
Breaking sound as varied in tone
As bass, bassoon, and timpani.
When the music reaches my inner ear,
When the chill wind's behind me on the bay
Where sun and mist mingle, I'm running free.